One Day

Suma Din · Illustrated by Christiane Engel

A & C BLACK
AN IMPRINT OF BLOOMSBURY
LONDON NEW DELHI NEW YORK SYDNEY

Published 2013 by
A&C Black
an imprint of Bloomsbury Publishing Plc
50 Bedford Square, London, WC1B 3DP
www.bloomsbury.com

ISBN HB 978-1-4081-8023-5
ISBN PB 978-1-4081-8024-2

This book is produced using paper that is made from wood grown in managed, sustainable forests.
It is natural, renewable and recyclable. The logging and manufacturing processes conform to the
environmental regulations of the country of origin.

Printed in China by Toppan Leefung.

10 9 8 7 6 5 4 3 2 1
10 9 8 7 6 5 4 3 2 1

MIX
Paper from
responsible sources
FSC
www.fsc.org FSC® C104723

Acknowledgments

I'd like to thank some special people who helped to turn a head-spinning idea into the book in your
hands. Starting with the youngest helpers: Maryam and Haala Khan for talking and thinking about
my fifteen children like they are real; Mudassir Mirza for her guidance on the topic of 'time' in
primary schools and Zilola Murtullayeva for giving me a flavour of Uzbek culture. I am indebted to
Elizabeth Jenner, for her insights, advice and belief in the idea from its inception. Thank you to the
illustrator Christiane Engel for making the world inside One Day so vivid and authentic.

Special thank you to Ibrahim Hamid, my son and partner in 'time'. This book grew out of our
discussions on what children in different time zones were doing while he was going about his day. In
the time that's passed between the ideas and the publication of this book, he's moved from primary
to secondary school but has always stayed interested and involved.

One Day

Time for school, time for lunch, time for your friend to arrive... there's always someone talking about time!

But have you ever thought about what a child in South Africa is doing when you're waking up? Maybe you've wondered what a child in Australia is doing when you're eating your breakfast. And where in the world do children wake up just as you're going to bed?

One Day will give you some answers. Follow fifteen children through their day and night and see what they all get up to. While Victor's fishing in Peru, Mani is walking all the way to his uncle's house in DR Congo. At the same time, Paige is looking out for the Southern star at night in Australia and Chica's baking sweet bread after school in Portugal.

Find out what happens to them and all the other children when you spend One Day with them!

Meet the children around the world

Here are all the children and the time zones they live in. There are 24 hours in a day, so there are 24 time zones. Which time zone do you live in?

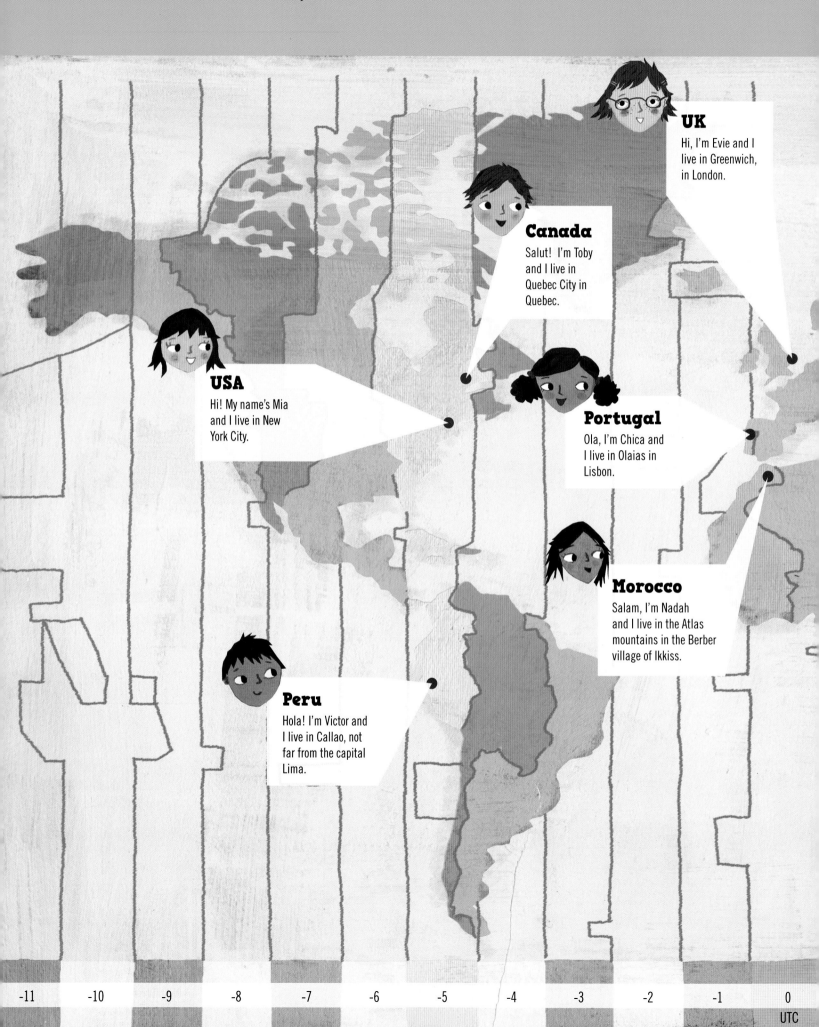

UK

Hi, I'm Evie and I live in Greenwich, in London.

Canada

Salut! I'm Toby and I live in Quebec City in Quebec.

USA

Hi! My name's Mia and I live in New York City.

Portugal

Ola, I'm Chica and I live in Olaias in Lisbon.

Morocco

Salam, I'm Nadah and I live in the Atlas mountains in the Berber village of Ikkiss.

Peru

Hola! I'm Victor and I live in Callao, not far from the capital Lima.

-11	-10	-9	-8	-7	-6	-5	-4	-3	-2	-1	0

UTC

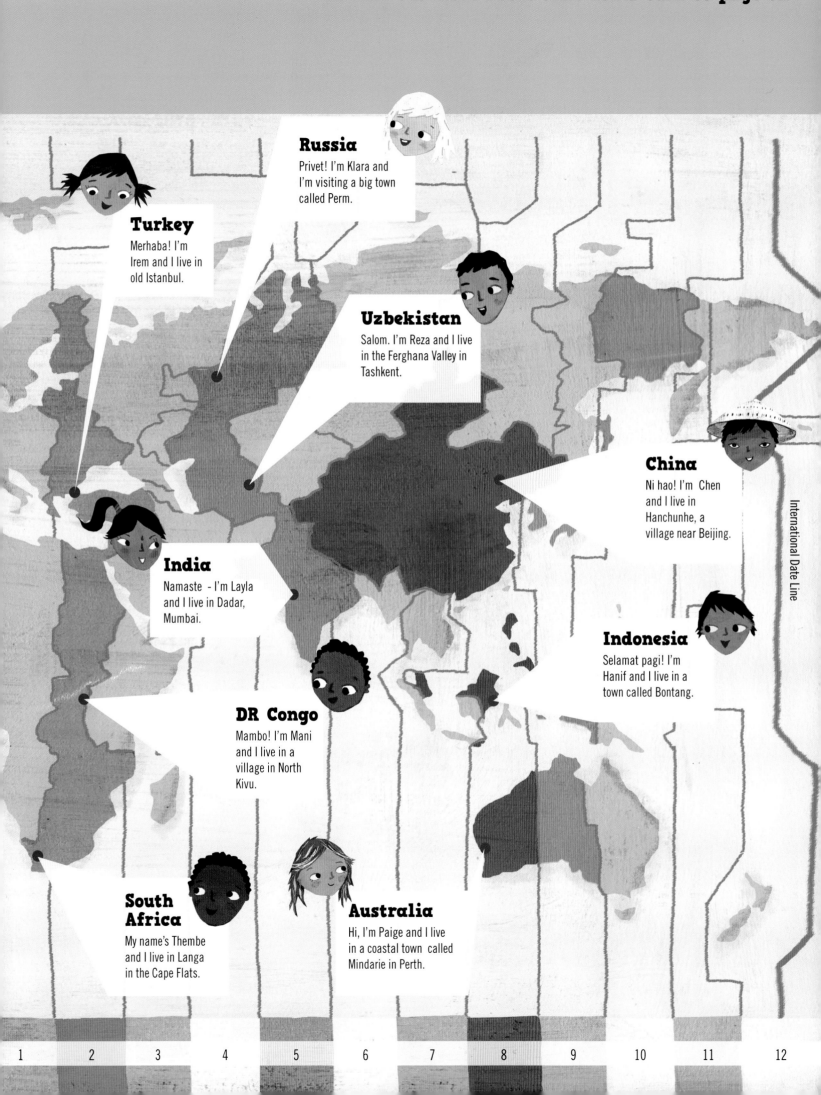

Turkey

Merhaba! I'm Irem and I live in old Istanbul.

Russia

Privet! I'm Klara and I'm visiting a big town called Perm.

Uzbekistan

Salom. I'm Reza and I live in the Ferghana Valley in Tashkent.

China

Ni hao! I'm Chen and I live in Hanchunhe, a village near Beijing.

India

Namaste - I'm Layla and I live in Dadar, Mumbai.

Indonesia

Selamat pagi! I'm Hanif and I live in a town called Bontang.

DR Congo

Mambo! I'm Mani and I live in a village in North Kivu.

South Africa

My name's Thembe and I live in Langa in the Cape Flats.

Australia

Hi, I'm Paige and I live in a coastal town called Mindarie in Perth.

International Date Line

1   2   3   4   5   6   7   8   9   10   11   12

UK 07.00

Evie jumps out of bed and starts to get ready for school. She puts her uniform on and quickly eats some cereal and orange juice for breakfast. She's playing in the big school football match today and she can't wait to get there!

South Africa 09.00

Thembe's at school in his first lesson, Geography. He's making a poster about the most common fruits grown in South Africa, like pineapples, pears, grapes, guavas, papayas and mangos. Miss Julie has told him to work with Kayla – his enemy. 'You colour and I'll draw,' she orders.

USA 02.00

In the middle of the night, all the lights are off in Mia's apartment. Mia's falling asleep in bed and Coco, her cat, is fast asleep in his basket. Outside, the subway trains, taxis and buses are still running.

India 12.30

Layla's in her last lesson at school before lunch time. She starts to daydream. The neem tree in the schoolyard looks like it's sizzling. She jumps as her teacher puts a piece of paper on her desk. '10/10 for your Hindi test, Layla. Well done.'

China 15.00

Chen's day at school is over. He walks home to his grandmother Nai Nai's farm and helps with the garlic and celery harvest. He loves talking to Nai Nai when they're out together. He's telling her about the kite he's made at school.

Capital: Beijing
Total Area: 9,596,961 sq km
Population: 1,343,239,923
Currency: renminbi (also known as the yuan)
Official Language: Mandarin Chinese

08.00 09.00 10.00 11.00 12.00 13.00 14.00 15.00 16.00 17.00 18.00 19.00

Uzbekistan 14.00

School has just finished for today. Reza races out to his friend's house. All the boys are eager to see his friend's new horse. He takes a short cut along the side of the cotton field.

Capital: Tashkent
Total Area: 447,400 sq km
Population: 28,394,180
Currency: Uzbek som (UZS)
Official Language: Uzbek

22.00   23.00   24.00   01.00   02.00   03.00   04.00   05.00   06.00   07.00   08.00   09.00

Portugal 09.00

Chica has taken the tram to school and is now in her first lesson, Spanish. They are writing letters to children in another school far away, in Puerto Rico. 'I'm ready to write my email,' Chica says to her teacher. 'It's all about the big surprise I'm waiting for.'

Peru 04.00

Victor stirs from his sleep. He hears a creak as the wooden door shuts. He opens his eyes to see Grandma, Grandpa and Mama fast asleep. Papi must have left to go to the harbour – he's a fisherman and his day starts early. I wish I could go too, he thinks to himself. But he knows if he moves now, his mother will catch him.

DR Congo 11.00

Mani, his mother and baby brother are still on the road. They have been walking for two days now. They left their village in the middle of the night. Mani is exhausted and asks the roadside pineapple seller for some water. 'Just a few more hours till we reach the farm,' Mama tells him.

Australia 17.00

Paige and her family have just arrived at their beach house in the Marina to spend the weekend with her cousins. Paige loves the ocean. But she's got to keep an eye out for sea urchins in the water that sting.

Morocco 11.00

Nadah is in a Maths lesson with her older sister and younger friends. The teacher is writing on the blackboard, but Nadah can't concentrate today. She can see her family's herd of goats from the window. They've just returned from grazing by the spring. Nadah's thinking about her favourite goat – Sifee.

Canada 06.00

Toby is waking up. It's the day of his school trip to the Colisee Pepsi – the largest Junior hockey arena in the world. Toby's excited about seeing more of Quebec City, as his family have just moved here. He hears Dad going out of the house through the snow to his early shift in the bakery.

Russia 16.00

Klara and her father have just arrived at Perm City station, a long way from their village. It was a great adventure travelling on the Siberian Express, seeing so many towns and bridges. They have come to visit Klara's aunt in Perm. Klara spots her on the platform.
'There she is!'

Indonesia 19.00

It's Hanif's favourite time of the day – dinner time. His grandmother has come to visit. She's brought a jack fruit, coconut and homemade snacks. Hanif loves his grandma's cooking. He helps his mother serve the big family meal of rice, fish, peanut sauce and vegetables.

Turkey 13.00

Irem's at school in an Art lesson. She's happily washing her paper with special paint to make *Ebru* designs. Miss Ela showed them hers first. Irem can't wait to show Grandpa her art when she visits him in the evening.

Capital: Ankara
Population: 79,749,461
Total Area: 780,562 sq km
Currency: Turkish lira (TRL)
Official Language: Turkish

UK 13.00

It's the inter-house football match and Evie's standing in the goal – ready and waiting. The ball's heading towards her and she dives towards it. Her friends cheer her on from the sidelines. Lessons have been cancelled this afternoon so everyone can watch the tournament.

Capital: London (England)
Population: 63,047,162
Total Area: 243,122 sq km
Currency: British pound (GBP)
Official Language: English

USA 08.00

Mia has finished her breakfast pancakes and has a long list of jobs to help with. There's no time to waste! Coco needs to go next door to their neighbour, Mrs Jones. Mom's carrying his food and favourite water bowl. 'I'll miss you Coco,' Mia says, as she hands him over.

South Africa 15.00

The school day has just finished, and Thembe has gone next door to the community centre where there's a football club. He's playing with his friends and waiting for the coach to arrive. Oh no, who does he see in the yard? It's Kayla, again.

India 18.30

Layla's making a bracelet on the balcony when she hears "Psst, Layla... it's me!" She peeks through the frame and sees Suraj, who lives behind her apartment. 'Ssh,' she whispers back. She creeps past her snoring grandmother, down the stairs, and gives a package to him. 'It's sandwiches and pencils.'

China 21.00

Chen and his grandmother are eating candied yams. She is telling him a story about the special silk kite she had when she was a young girl. She had many adventures flying it near the old temple in her village. 'Just one more story, please, Nai Nai,' Chen says. But Nai Nai isn't feeling well. 'No more today. Your mama and baba will be back from work any minute now. Off to bed!'

| 14.00 | 15.00 | 16.00 | 17.00 | 18.00 | 19.00 | 20.00 | 21.00 | 22.00 | 23.00 | 24.00 | 01.00 |

Peru 10.00

Victor and his friends have gone to the bay instead of going to school. They are having fun splashing about and fishing. 'Look what I've caught!' Victor shouts to his friends. 'Oh no, look who's coming!' they yell as they begin to run. Victor's mother has arrived.

DR Congo 17.00

Mani, Mama and his brother have reached Uncle Obi's house, and are eating stew and *fufu*. Mama tells Uncle Obi about the troubles in their village. She cries when she describes the fire that destroyed all their neighbours' houses.

Uzbekistan 20.00

Reza and his family have just finished their evening meal, cooked by his mother and his aunts. They had *palov*, stewed vegetables and watermelon afterwards. He's telling everyone all about his friend's new horse. 'It's a beautiful brown mare and I even got to ride it', he boasts to his older brothers and sisters.

Australia 23.00

The moonlight shines through the beach house window, across Paige's bed. The sea and sky look like a speckled blanket that go on forever. She's trying to spot the Southern Cross stars, like the ones on the Australian flag in her room.

04.00   05.00   06.00   07.00   08.00   09.00   10.00   11.00   12.00   13.00   14.00   15.00

Portugal 15.00

Chica is back from school now and helps her mother bake some sweet bread, which is called *pão doce*. Her neighbour Ellena comes over to play and has brought her spinning tops for a competition, after they eat some sweet bread.

Capital: Lisbon
Population: 10,781,459
Total Area: 92,090 sq km
Currency: euro (EUR)
Official Language: Portuguese

Morocco 17.00

The evening gets cool and there's nobody outside amongst the olive grove and almond trees. Nadah's mama has baked fresh bread and made soup. It smells tasty. Her family sit close to the fire while they eat their soup. Nadah finishes first. 'Papa, can I go and see my goat Sifee again?'

Turkey 19.00

Irem's grandfather is taking her and her little brother Mert to buy some Turkish sweets from his friend's shop. Mert loves the hardboiled sweets and all the kinds of chewy soft *locum*. They weave through the crowded spice market lit by multi-coloured lanterns, with the tangy smell in the air. Irem turns around to hold Mert's hand… but where's he gone?

Indonesia 01.00

Hanif is fast asleep under the mosquito net. It's monsoon season and outside the rain is pouring down hard. The rainwater makes all the streets around Hanif's house shimmer in the moonlight.

Canada 12.00

Toby's class are walking around the Colisée. They're looking at pictures of famous teams that have played ice hockey there. 'Who wants to buy a souvenir?' asks Miss Perrier.

Capital: Ottawa
Population: 34,300,083
Total Area: 9,984,670 sq km
Currency: Canadian dollar (CAD)
Official Languages: French/English

Russia 22.00

Klara, her father and her aunt all had a brilliant time at the circus. She loved the trapeze act with the amazing acrobat whizzing high up in the tent. 'But the bears and the white horses were my favourite. Thank you, Aunty!' she says as her aunt gives her a hot chocolate drink before bed.

Capital: Moscow
Population: 138,082,178
Total Area: 17,098,242 sq km
Currency: Russian rouble (RUR)
Official Language: Russian

UK 19.00

Evie is eating fish and chips when her father gets home from work. 'Dad, we won the match!' Evie tells her father. 'Fantastic,' Dad says. 'What a great way to start the weekend.' 'Are we going anywhere tomorrow, Dad?' 'We are, but it's a surprise. We have to leave early tomorrow morning.'

India 00.30

Layla's asleep, and her neighbour Suraj is trying out the pencils. Even though he's only 7 years old, he's been working all evening with his mother – selling puffed rice outside the cinema hall. He's staying up late to trace Layla's handwriting, going over and over words in her old book.

China 03.00

Everyone's asleep apart from Chen's grandmother, Nai Nai. She's not feeling well and calls out to Chen's mama, 'I'm finding it hard to breathe.' Baba decides she has to go to the village hospital nearby. He drives her through the soundless roads around their villa, and they arrive in ten minutes.

08.00   09.00   10.00   11.00   12.00   13.00   14.00   15.00   16.00   17.00   18.00   19.00

USA 14.00

Mia's handbag is packed - the DS, her earphones, two games, a pack of cards and all her sweets. What's that in the corner? She notices Coco the cat's basket and toys on the landing. 'Mom, we forgot to give Mrs Jones the basket. Shall I take it next door?' Another chance to say goodbye to him!

Capital: Washington, DC
Population: 313,847,465
Total Area: 9,826,675 sq km
Currency: US dollar
Official Language: English

South Africa 21.00

Thembe's tired from football practice. He tries to sleep. His brothers are snoring next to him and his cousin is listening to the radio. He hears his mother locking up the windows of their *spaza* shop next door. Thembe's mum and dad sell everything from toothpaste to teabags in their colourful shop.

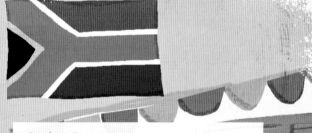

Capital: Pretoria
Population: 48,810,427
Total Area: 1,219,090 sq km
Currency: rand (ZAR)
Official Languages: English/Afrikaans and 9 other officially recognised languages

Portugal 21.00

After a family dinner of grilled fish and boiled potatoes, Chica's gone to sleep. Her mum wakes her up gently. 'We're off to the hospital, sweetheart. Your sister's downstairs. Sleep well.' Her mum and dad drive away soon after.

DR Congo 23.00

Mani is sleeping in Uncle Obi's house, next to his cousins. He dreams about his village he has left behind. He used to love selling the sweet pies and fried plantain made by his mother in the market. He misses his ducks and the neighbours and wishes he could go back home.

Uzbekistan 02.00

All of Reza's family are fast asleep. Only Reza's older brother is out on the night patrol, because he's training to be a policeman. He has to be careful as there's often trouble in the town at night.

10.00   11.00   12.00   13.00   14.00   15.00   16.00   17.00   18.00   19.00   20.00   21.00

Peru 16.00

Victor is sitting in front of his mother with his school books. His sisters are outside playing, but he is not allowed out because he skipped school. His reading book is open, but his eyes are on the colourful patterns Mama is weaving

Capital: Lima
Population: 29,549,517
Total Area: 1,285,216 sq km
Currency: nuevo sol (PEN)
Official Languages: Spanish/Aymara/Quechua

Australia 05.00

Paige is sound asleep. But the pelicans and seagulls are wide awake, squawking and chattering at dawn. It sounds like they're talking about Paige's cousins out for their early morning surf.

Capital: Canberra
Population: 22,158,576
Total Area: 7,692,024 sq km
Currency: Australian dollar (AUD)
Official Language: English

22.00   23.00   24.00   01.00   02.00   03.00   04.00   05.00   06.00   07.00   08.00   09.00

Morocco 23.00

All the fires are out and the village is fast asleep. Nadah's asleep on the mattress next to her aunt and sister. But Sifee the goat is awake, standing under the starlit sky, stretching and braying. Papa hears the braying and creeps out of the house, ever so quietly.

Capital: Rabat
Population: 32,309,239
Total Area: 446,550 sq km
Currency: Moroccan dirham (MAD)
Official Language: Arabic

12.00   13.00   14.00   15.00   16.00   17.00   18.00   19.00   20.00   21.00   22.00   23.00

Canada 18.00

Toby's at home telling his mum and dad all about his school trip. 'What did you see on the way there?' asks his mum. 'We went past Notre Dame de Quebec Cathedral and a place called the 'citadel'. Can we go there?'

Turkey 01.00

Irem's back home and fast asleep. She's exhausted from searching for Mert with her grandfather. They looked everywhere. After two hours, they finally found him in a pastry shop!

Indonesia 07.00

Hanif is awake and opens the window. He feels the steamy warm air rising over the puddles of water outside. It's too wet to play outside so he wakes his sister up. 'Do you want to play cards? Wake up!'

Russia 04.00

Klara wakes up again. She's been tossing and turning every time a lorry goes by. There are bright lights shining from a factory through the curtain too. Her aunt's house in Perm is not like home. Back in their *dacha*, it's quiet and everything's still all night long. The only sound is the owl hooting.

| 24.00 | 01.00 | 02.00 | 03.00 | 04.00 | 05.00 | 06.00 | 07.00 | 08.00 | 09.00 | 10.00 | 11.00 |

India 06.30

Layla's awake early today. She's practising her exercises before she goes to her morning Kathak dance class. Dadima has already started cooking aubergine, cauliflower and okra and fills the house with a spicy aroma. Layla can't wait to show her new moves to her friends when she goes back to school on Monday.

Capital: New Delhi
Population: 1,205,073,612 (2012 est)
Total Area: 3,287,263 sq km
Currency: Indian rupee (INR)
Official Languages: Hindi/English

| 14.00 | 15.00 | 16.00 | 17.00 | 18.00 | 19.00 | 20.00 | 21.00 | 22.00 | 23.00 | 24.00 | 01.00 |

UK 01.00

Evie's dreaming about where they could be going in the morning. Could it be a trip to see her favourite football team play a match? Or maybe a surprise holiday to somewhere sunny and hot? She loves going to Spain in the summer, to spend time at the beach.

USA 20.00

It's take-off time! Mia and her mom reached JFK airport just in time and now the plane's about to fly. Mia peers out of the window and watches New York City become smaller and smaller as they rise higher and higher in the sky.

China 09.00

Chen wakes up and looks for Baba. Mama tells him what happened during the night. 'Don't worry, we'll go to the hospital this afternoon. She needs another day of rest.' But Chen is worried. He goes to his room to finish the kite he's going to give Nai Nai.

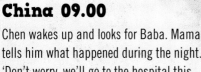

South Africa 03.00

Crash! Bang! What's going on outside? Thembe sits up in bed, frozen with fright. A police car siren can be heard in the distance and two oil cans roll down the alleyway. Papa looks out of the window and sees neighbours peering out of their windows too. 'Go back to sleep everyone… it's just Danny. He's knocked a paint can over!'

02.00 03.00 04.00 05.00 06.00 07.00 08.00 09.00 10.00 11.00 12.00 13.00

Portugal 03.00

'Chica, Chica,' her big sister whispers, 'we've got a baby brother!' But Chica's too sleepy to hear her sister, who creeps out the room and gently closes the door. She's so excited that she decides to ring her padrinhos – her godparents – and tell them the news!

Peru 22.00

Victor's father is proud of the huge fish Victor caught. 'This will be delicious!' he tells Mama when he finishes cleaning it. Victor hears him and feels a bit happier before he falls asleep. Maybe getting in trouble was worth it after all.

Uzbekistan 08.00

Reza's mother has made fresh bread in the *tandoor* for breakfast. As it's the weekend, they have a big breakfast which includes a delicious home-made clotted cream and green tea with lots of sugar!

Australia 11.00

Paige helps Mum clear up after their delicious brunch. They had sausages, eggs, baked beans and toast. She's looking for the Anzac biscuits. It looks like the seagulls are looking too! Next, Paige and her cousins get ready for a game of beach volleyball.

DR Congo 05.00

'Mani, I'm going out to the fields.' Mama says. 'Look after
your brother and don't cause any trouble. I'll be back in
the afternoon.' She is going out to work on the cassava
plantations. Mani nods at his mother and falls asleep again.
He wants to carry on dreaming.

Capital: Kinshasa
Population: 73,599,190
Total Area: 2,344,858 sq km
Currency: Congolese francs
Official Language: French

| 04.00 | 05.00 | 06.00 | 07.00 | 08.00 | 09.00 | 10.00 | 11.00 | 12.00 | 13.00 | 14.00 | 15.00 |

Morocco 05.00

The rooster crows its croaky *cock-a-doodle-doo* and Nadah scrambles up and peers out of the window. She can see Mama starting up the hill to collect water. She pulls her blanket around her and runs outside to see her favourite goat, Sifee. 'Papa, she's had three babies!' she calls out.

Canada 24.00

Toby is asleep now. He's put the souvenir from today's school trip on his bookshelf. It's a hockey puck. It's next to his favourite Tintin book 'Explorers on the Moon'. Tomorrow he'll be exploring Quebec's citadel with his parents, climbing high up to see the sights of their new home city.

Turkey 07.00

Irem wakes up to the smell of freshly baked *pide*, feta cheese and olives. She creeps across the bedroom to the bathroom. Mert is still asleep. She's the first in the kitchen for breakfast, dipping the warm bread in olive oil.

Russia 10.00

'Wake up,' says Klara's father, 'you've slept for half of the morning!' 'What are we doing today?' Klara asks, with a wide yawn. 'After your breakfast, we're going to the Kungur Ice Caves. You'll love them – there are hundreds of grottos.'

18.00   19.00   20.00   21.00   22.00   23.00   24.00   01.00   02.00   03.00   04.00   05.00

Indonesia 13.00

The sun's rays have brought out Hanif's friends. He can hear their voices and the sloshing sound of their boots as they run towards his house. Hanif is soon out to join them. Their houses are built on stilts so the monsoon showers don't flood their homes. They have fun splashing in the huge puddles and floating twigs in the stream.

Capital: Jakarta
Population: 248,216,193
Total Area: 1,904,569 sq km
Currency: Indonesian rupiah (IDR)
Official Language: Bahasa Indonesian

06.00   07.00   08.00   09.00   10.00   11.00   12.00   13.00   14.00   15.00   16.00   17.00

England 07.00 (USA 02.00)

Evie and her parents have woken up very early to drive to the airport. Evie wants to know what the surprise is, but Mum and Dad won't tell. 'Look,' Dad says, pointing, 'who's that over there?' Evie gasps. 'It's Aunty Olivia and Mia from New York! So THAT's the surprise!'

| 20.00 | 21.00 | 22.00 | 23.00 | 24.00 | 01.00 | 02.00 | 03.00 | 04.00 | 05.00 | 06.00 | 07.00 |

If you want to know more about time...

What is a time zone?

People living in different places around the world will all have watches saying different times. Their watches tell different times because they live in different time zones – 24 to be exact!

Time zones occur because the Earth doesn't stay still. It's always turning, very slowly. When it turns, the part of the Earth that is near the sun has daylight hours. At the same time, the opposite part of the Earth is in darkness, so it's night time there. In between day time and night time, there are all the other times of the day; dawn, sunrise, afternoon, evening and dusk, as that part of the Earth moves closer or further away from the sun.

As it takes the Earth 24 hours to rotate (turn a full circle), there are 24 time zones. The time zones are at equal distances from each other. Small countries fall into one of the time zones depending on where they are in the world. Some larger countries have two, three or four time zones as they are so big.

On maps and diagrams, like the one on pages 4-5, time zones are marked by long lines going from the North Pole to the South Pole. These lines are known as lines of longitude.

Long ago...

Time has always been important to us! Before there were no clocks, computers or mobile phones, people still wanted to know what the time was. They used sundials, water and sand devices to measure time. The position of the sun was very important in working out what the time was.

Using the sun to tell the time had some problems. Firstly, the movement of the sun across the sky varies slightly over the year, and secondly, the position of the sun in the sky varies from place to place, which caused cities near to each other to have different times.

To solve all these problems, an average time was worked out from looking at all the sundial days in the year. Another word for average is 'mean', which is where the term 'mean time' comes from.

Greenwich

In order to have all the clocks telling the same time, the town of Greenwich, in London, UK, was chosen as a central point to measure time for all other places in the world.

Greenwich is where the Royal Observatory was built in 1675. They used huge telescopes to calculate the mean time – which became world-famous as 'Greenwich Mean Time'. A solid metal line in the concrete just outside the observatory, known as the 'Meridian' is where all distances to the East (on the right side of the line) and to the West (on the left side of the line) are measured from.

In 1884, representatives from 25 countries met in Washington DC, USA, for a meeting called 'The International Meridian Conference'. At the meeting, there was a vote for which country should be chosen as the one standard place to measure time for the whole world. Greenwich won the vote. Its Meridian line was decided to be the place from which all time around the world would be measured. This international standard was known as GMT – Greenwich Mean Time.

Universal Coordinated Time

But measuring time wasn't that simple! As technology improved, it was found that measuring time could be even more exact.

70 national time laboratories around the world had clocks measuring time down to the millisecond. In 1961, the International Radio Consultative Committee decided to use the average time of these 70 laboratories as the standard time across the world – to be known as Universal Coordinated Time (UTC). People still use GMT when talking about time in another country, but for pilots, the navy, and world trade and business, universal coordinated time is now used instead.

Glossary

baba – dad
dacha – a countryside house in Russia
DS – a portable electronic game
Ebru – a Turkish art, using inks and water to make marbled paper
fufu – an African dish made from boiling vegetables into a paste
Hindi – the national language of India
jack fruit – a large fruit with a prickly shell on the outside and yellow soft pods inside. Found in tropical countries
locum – Turkish Delight, a sweet
monsoon – the summer rainy season in Asian countries
nai nai – Mandarin Chinese for grandma (on father's side of the family)
neem – a popular tree found in towns all over India
palov – a national dish made of rice, meat and carrots and vegetables in Uzbekistan
pão doce – a sweet bread made with sugar or honey in Portugal
pide – Turkish bread
plantain – a tropical fruit similar to a banana
sea urchin – a small sea animal with a hard shell covered in sharp points
spaza shop – South African slang for a small general store in townships
tandoor – a clay oven used for cooking in parts of Asia